Farm Animals

PIGS

Rachael Bell

Heinemann
LIBRARY

www.heinemann.co.uk
Visit our website to find out more information about Heinemann Library books.

To order:

☎ Phone 44 (0) 1865 888066

▤ Send a fax to 44 (0) 1865 314091

▥ Visit the Heinemann Bookshop at www.heinemann.co.uk to browse our catalogue and order online.

First published in Great Britain by Heinemann Library,
Halley Court, Jordan Hill, Oxford OX2 8EJ,
a division of Reed Educational and Professional Publishing Ltd.
Heinemann is a registered trademark of Reed Educational and Professional Publishing Ltd.

OXFORD MELBOURNE AUCKLAND
JOHANNESBURG BLANTYRE GABORONE
IBADAN PORTSMOUTH (NH) USA CHICAGO

Designed by AMR
Originated by Ambassador Litho ltd
Printed by South China Printing in Hong Kong/China

ISBN 0 431 13330 1 (hardback)   ISBN 0 431 13335 2 (paperback)
05 04 03 02 01   05 04 03 02 01
10 9 8 7 6 5 4 3 2 1   10 9 8 7 6 5 4 3 2 1

British Library Cataloguing in Publication Data

Bell, Rachael, 1972–
  Pigs. – (Farm animals) (Take-off!)
  1.Swine – Juvenile literature
  I.Title
  636.4

Acknowledgements

The publishers would like to thank the following for permission to reproduce photographs: Agripicture/Peter Dean pp 6; Farmers Weekly Picture Library pp 8, 13, 18, 20; Garden Matters pp 12 & 16/John Phipps; Holt Studios pp 4 t, 14 & 28 b/Sarah Rowland, 4 b,10, 11, & 24/Nigel Cattlin, 25/Gordon Roberts; Chris Honeywell p 22, 27; Images of Nature/FLPA pp 5/Silvestris, 9/E & D Hosking, 15/J. C. Allen, 17/Peter Dean, 26/M. Nimmo; NHPA p 19/B. A. Janes; d. b. Pineider p 23; Lynn M Stone p 28 t; Tony Stone Images pp 7/H. Richard Johnston, 21/Andy Sacks.

Cover photograph reproduced with permission of NHPA.

Our thanks to Sue Graves and Hilda Reed for their advice and expertise in the preparation of this book.

Every effort has been made to contact copyright holders of any material reproduced in this book. Any omissions will be rectified in subsequent printings if notice is given to the publishers.

Contents

Any words appearing in the text in bold, **like this**, are explained in the Glossary.

What do pigs look like?

Gloucester Old Spot

Most pig farmers keep large, pink pigs like this.

Most pig farmers keep large, pink pigs. These grow well and have lots of baby pigs. Other kinds of pigs, such as the Gloucester Old Spot, do not grow so quickly. They look interesting because of their unusual markings.

dark, hairy coat

Wild boars can be found in some forests.

Wild pigs are called wild **boars**. They live in some forests and can be fierce. They are smaller than farm pigs. Their coats are darker and more hairy.

Farm pigs are descended from wild boars.

On the pig farm

There are cows as well as pigs on this farm.

pigs

cows

On this pig farm, the farmer keeps pigs and a few cows. The only other animals on the farm are two pet dogs.

People first began to keep pigs in pens 9000 years ago!

Much of the land on a pig farm is used for growing crops like this.

Although this is a pig farm, much of the land is used for growing **crops** like wheat or barley. Some of the wheat and barley is **milled** and fed to the pigs.

Adult pigs

ears

tail

snout

trotter
(four
toes)

teat

udder

A sow eats a lot of food every day.

Female pigs are called **sows**. They eat lots of food to make milk to feed their **piglets**. Some sows eat 10 kilograms of food every day.

Very young female pigs are called gilts. They are called sows once they have had piglets.

A boar eats less than a sow.

tusk

Male pigs are called **boars**. They can weigh nearly three times as much as a man! They eat less than sows, but they fight more, using their **tusks**.

Pigs drink lots of water. They drink up to 9 litres of water a day.

Young pigs

Each of these piglets weighs about 1 kilogram.

piglet

A baby pig is called a **piglet**. It can walk almost as soon as it is born. It weighs about 1 kilogram, the same as a bag of sugar.

Piglets are usually born 16 weeks after mating.

sow

piglets

The piglets drink their mother's milk.

Sows usually have about eleven piglets in each **litter**. The sow makes the piglets feed regularly. About three times every hour, she grunts to call them to feed from her.

Piglets only drink their mother's milk for about three weeks after they are born.

11

Where are pigs kept?

These pigs live in indoor pens.

straw bedding

pigs

On this farm, the pigs live in indoor **pens**. They have **straw bedding** to keep them clean and warm. The straw is changed every two days.

The pigs eat from a special feed trough.

feed trough

The pigs lie in one area that is warm and dry. They get up to eat in the other area, where there is a feed **trough** and a **water drinker**.

What do pigs eat?

Pigs eat a lot of food that is made from plants.

Pigs can bite, chew and drink. They eat meat and plants. Most pig food is made from plants, and is a bit like breakfast cereal.

feed **trough**

piglets

These piglets are old enough to eat special pellets now.

When they are three weeks old, the **piglets** leave their mother. They eat special **pellets**. Older pigs eat liquid food, like thick soup. This is easy to feed to lots of pigs.

How do pigs stay healthy?

Pigs like to live and play together.

Pigs like to play-fight with each other. This is good exercise and helps them to keep fit. It also helps them to find out their **pecking order**.

Farmers may cut off the points of a piglet's teeth so that it does not bite too hard when it plays.

wet mud

Pigs like to wallow in mud to keep cool.

Pigs like to **wallow** in wet mud or straw. This keeps them cool in hot weather. Some farms use water sprinklers to give them cold showers!

Pigs wallow in mud because they cannot sweat, like us, to keep cool.

How do pigs sleep?

Pigs like to sleep in nests of straw during the main part of the day.

straw nest

Pigs are most active at dawn, when the sun comes up, or at dusk, when it goes down. Between these times, they sleep in nests made in their straw.

Pigs like to sleep very close to each other.

When a pig sleeps, it likes to lie on its side with its legs out straight. Pigs sleep close to each other to keep warm.

Who looks after pigs?

farm worker

pens

pigs

These pigs are looked after by a farm worker.

On a large pig farm, several people look after the pigs. One person looks after the **sows** and young **piglets**, and someone else looks after the older piglets.

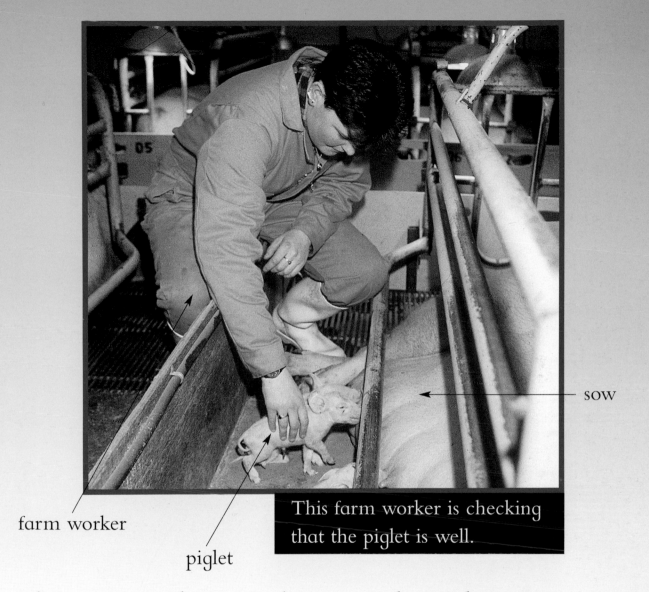

farm worker

sow

piglet

This farm worker is checking that the piglet is well.

This farm worker is making sure the piglets are well. Sometimes the **vet** is called when the pigs are ill.

A weak piglet is called a runt. Runts are often bottle-fed to help them survive.

What are pigs kept for?

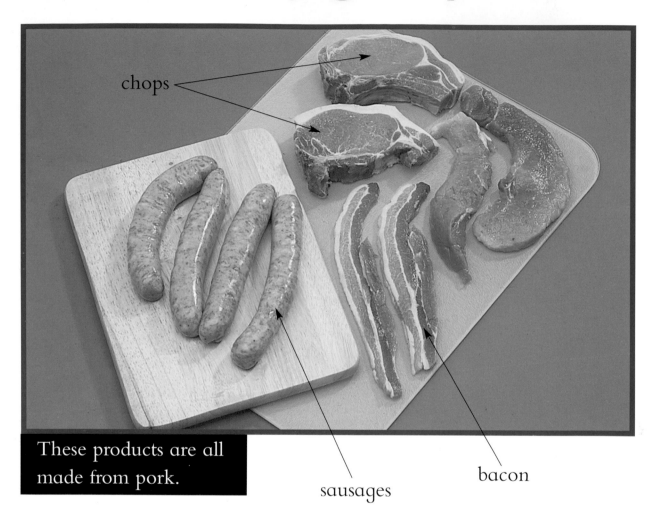

chops

These products are all made from pork.

sausages

bacon

People keeps pigs because we eat their meat, called pork. It is made into many different foods. Most sausages are made with **minced** pork. Bacon and ham are also made from pork.

tie case

photograph frame

All these things are made from pigskin.

credit card holder

key case

bag

purse

In some countries, pigskin is made into leather for making clothes and shoes. It feels very soft and smooth. Some brushes are made from pig **bristles**.

Other kinds of pig farm

shelter

These pigs live outside for most of the time.

On some pig farms, the pigs spend most of their time outdoors in a field. Their food is scattered on the ground. They go into their huts for shelter.

Pigs can get sunstroke so they need a shady place to shelter from the sun.

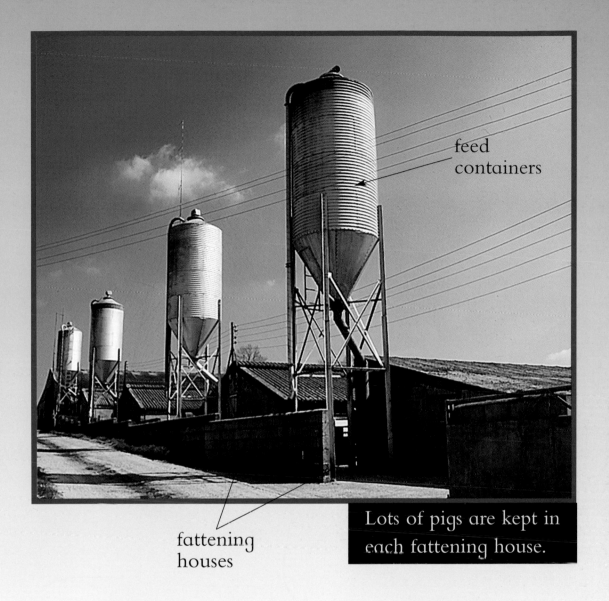

feed
containers

fattening
houses

Lots of pigs are kept in each fattening house.

Other pig farms keep their pigs in large buildings called fattening houses. The pigs get fat faster indoors than outdoors.

Organic pig farms

These pigs are organic pigs.

pigs

trees for shade

A few pig farms **rear** organic pigs. This means that the food that the pigs are given to eat does not contain any **drugs** to make them grow faster. Most organic pigs live outside.

Pigs that are not organic are given food with drugs added to it to make them grow faster.

pork chop

Some people prefer the taste of organic pork.

The meat from organic pigs costs more than ordinary pork because the pigs grow more slowly and the farmer has to look after them for longer. Some people think this pork tastes better.

Factfile

A **piglet** doubles its weight every week.

piglets

A **sow** can have 35 piglets a year.

A sow can only feed 12 piglets at a time because she only has 12 **teats**.

boar

If a sow has more than 12 piglets, another sow has to help feed them.

Some **boars** weigh as much as a small car!

In the wild, pigs find food by rooting around the ground with their snout. Pigs in the wild like to eat acorns and nuts.

Pigs have a good sense of smell. In France and northern Italy, farmers train their pigs to smell out **truffles**.

 Most of a pig can be eaten, even the **trotters**. Farmers used to say that the only thing you could not eat from a pig was its squeak!

Glossary

a
b
c
d
e
f
g
h
i
j
k
l
m
n
o
p
q
r
s
t
u
v
w
x
y
z

bedding   usually straw, for pigs to lie on

boar   male or father pig. Also the name for a wild pig.

bristles   the whiskers and short, stiff hairs

crops   plants farmers grow in their fields

drugs   special tablets or liquids given to pigs to keep them well and make them grow fast

female   girl or mother animal

joints   legs or shoulders of an animal

litter   group of animals born together from one mother

male   boy or father animal

milled   ground up

minced   chopped up finely or put through a mincer

pecking order   the order that shows which pig is more important than another

pellets   dry pig food that has been mixed and then pressed into tiny pieces

pen   room that pigs live in

piglet   young pig

rear   bring up young children or animals

sow	female or mother pig
snout	nose and mouth
teats	mouth pieces on the sow's milk bag that the piglets suck from
trotters	feet of a pig
trough	big food holder that the pigs eat from
truffles	special mushrooms that grow underground
tusks	the two large teeth that grow up out of the mouth of a boar
vet	doctor for animals
wallow	roll or lie in mud to keep cool
water drinker	type of water holder for pigs to drink from

a
b
c
d
e
f
g
h
i
j
k
l
m
n
o
p
q
r
s
t
u
v
w
x
y
z

More books to read

Babe the Sheep-pig,
Dick King-Smith, Longman

Charlotte's Web,
E.B. White, Puffin

Index